52

Object Lessons
for Students

Using Ordinary Items to Teach God's Word

SIDNEY LEASURE

52 Object Lessons for Students:
Using Ordinary Items to Teach God's Word

ISBN: 978-1-940645-77-3

COURIER PUBLISHING

Greenville, South Carolina

PRINTED IN THE UNITED STATES OF AMERICA

Introduction

This book was written in order to provide scriptural lessons to children and youth by using objects that can be found in any household. As a youth minister, I searched for a long time but could not find a book with object lessons using such easy-to-find items. So I decided to write my own.

The lessons are fun, but they send kids home thinking. Your students will be blindfolded and looking for a Snickers bar, or trying to put toothpaste back in a tube, or even having a texting contest. Each lesson is based in Scripture and geared to drive home the Word of God.

Each lesson should be finished by "going to the cross" and showing each student how everything leads to Jesus.

I pray this book will bless your ministry and help you lead one more young person to a saving knowledge of Jesus Christ.

Sidney Leasure
November 2019

Object Lesson

Hide a candy bar and then blindfold a student and ask him to find the candy bar. After he cannot find it, bring in a predetermined youth from outside the room and ask him to find the candy bar without a blindfold.

Point

After the second student finds it, explain that we need spiritual eyes to find heaven, and the Holy Spirit is the only way to see spiritually. Without the Holy Spirit, we are searching for heaven with blindfolds on our eyes. The way to see spiritually is by being born again. Go into detail about being born again.

Verse

John 3:1-8

Object Lesson

Divide the youth equally into two rooms. Let the youth talk to each other with a walkie-talkie set. After a while, turn off one of the walkie-talkies and let them try to communicate with each other. They will see there is communication from one walkie-talkie with no replies.

Point

God cannot speak to us if we are not turned on to hear His voice. We should be aware and always listening for His voice. We must be in a continuous state of prayer by keeping our walkie-talkie on so we can hear God whenever He decides to speak to us. This often can be done by being alone by ourselves in a quiet time.

Verse

I Thessalonians 5:17-18

Object Lesson

Bring two plates and then cut out pictures of food that comprise a hearty meal with a dessert. Place these food items on the first plate. Then on the other plate, place a picture of a cookie that represents a lesser meal.

Point

Our bodies need food to grow, or we will die. We cannot eat food as in the second example and expect our bodies to be in good shape. Likewise, our souls need spiritual nourishment. If they do not get the nourishment they need, our souls will likewise not be in good shape. We must read the Bible daily, just as we need to eat daily, to have a healthy soul that is fed from the Word of God.

Verse

Hebrews 5:12-14

Object Lesson

Put a plant in one can and some trash in another can, and then ask what each can is called. The students will reply, "A flower pot" and "a trash can." Swap the flower and trash from one can to the other, then pose the same question. The students will again call the can with the flower a flower pot and the can with the trash a trash can.

Point

Explain how the first can was called a flower pot when the flower was inside, but when you exchanged the flower with trash, they then called the same pot a trash can. Explain that we are the same way — that we become what we put inside ourselves. Whether it be dirty thoughts, movies with bad language, or music with bad lyrics, we are what we take in. We have to judge what we allow ourselves to become. You will take in what you love and reject what you hate.

Verse

Matthew 15:17-19

Object Lesson

Build an obstacle course with chairs in a small room. Take the youth through the room with the lights off. Then let them re-do the obstacle course with a flashlight.

Point

Explain that our journeys through life aren't easy or manageable without light. It is hard to maneuver in total darkness. But with light, we can see the obstacles in our path and make our way out. Explain how Jesus is the light unto our paths in life, and He will always guide us through life's obstacles and get us where we need to go.

Verse

John 11:9-10, Psalm 119:105

Object Lesson

Blindfold a student and ask him or her to find a certain person in the room. Then blindfold a different student and ask him or her to find this same person while the person is calling out to them.

Point

We are lost in life unless we listen and hear Jesus calling out to us. Jesus is our Shepherd, and no one can take us away from Him. There is nothing we can do to find Jesus with our works. We must find Jesus through His work, which is the cross. We must know that, through the cross, He is calling out to us for us to come to Him.

Verse

John 10:27-29

Object Lesson

Split the students into two groups. Make one team pass along the sentence "Jesus loves me" by lowly whispering to one another and see how the sentence changes at the end. Then make the other team pass along the same statement by speaking it out loud. See how the sentence that is whispered changes at the end, but the spoken sentence does not change.

Point

Without the spoken word, we cannot communicate with each other or get to know one another. The Holy Spirit is the spoken Word of God living in our hearts. We cannot know God without reading the Word of God. We must get into a daily schedule of reading our Bible.

Verse

John 1:1

Object Lesson

Bring three students into a room, one at a time, and ask them to sit on a chair. Then bring three blindfolded students into the room, one at a time, and lead them to a chair, asking them to sit on the chair unassisted.

Point

Point out the faith that the ones who could see had in the chair when they sat down: They all sat down quickly when they were told to, and they had complete faith in the chair holding them. Then point out how the three blindfolded ones acted differently when they could not physically see the chair: They felt the chair and then eased into the seat. Even though we cannot see God, we must have faith in Him — just like the ones who could see the chair.

Verse

John 20:29

Object Lesson

Get a student to sit in the floor and yell out for help as if he were drowning. Get two other students and instruct them to stand in front of the drowning victim and talk flippantly with no worries about the struggling victim. Have a student then run in with urgency and throw a rope out to the drowning victim, pulling him in to a make-believe shore and rescuing the person from certain death.

Point

We all have friends who are not saved and going to hell — and we must not sit and watch, but instead we must try to rescue them. By not telling our friends about Jesus, we are acting like the people did who were letting the boy drown with no concern for his life.

Verse

Matthew 28:18-20

Object Lesson

Boil some water in the church kitchen. Bring in a glass of water and a glass of ice cubes.

Point

Explain how the steam from the boiling water is similar to a spirit form like the Holy Spirit. Show how water is different from steam but is made to sustain life just as Christ does. Show how ice is also different and tell how it sustains temperature for drinks, just as God sustains us. Tell how water, steam and ice have the same molecular makeup, yet have different purposes — just as the Trinity is one, but also serves different purposes.

Tell why "us" is used in some of the verses.

Verse

Genesis 1:26, Genesis 3:22, Philippians 2:5-8, John 1:1, Acts 5:3-4, Colossians 2:9

Object Lesson

Take a rubber band and stretch it between your index finger and thumb, placing the rubber band against someone's skin. Then pop the person with the rubber band, pulling it back a little further away from the person's skin each time.

Point

After the illustration, tell everyone how the rubber band represents truth and how it does not hurt when it is placed along someone's skin. But each time the rubber band — or the truth — is stretched further, the rubber band (truth) hurts worse. Stress the importance of telling the truth and how God hates a lie.

Verse

Proverbs 6:16-19

Object Lesson

Bring in some mud and let two students muddy their hands. Then allow one of them to wash his hands. Next, put a peeled banana in front of both students and ask out loud, "Should both students be allowed to eat the banana with their hands?" The answer should be, "The student with dirty hands cannot eat, but the student with clean hands can." Then ask about the student with clean hands: His hands used to be dirty. Why should he be able to eat? They should reply, "Because now they are clean."

Point

Explain that God looks at us the same way when we accept Jesus Christ into our lives as our personal Savior. We are dirty from sin, but the blood of Jesus washes our dirt away and then we can come to God. But if we do not let Jesus wash away our dirt, then we are like the student who wanted to eat his banana with dirty hands. With Jesus, we are cleansed as if we were never dirty before.

Verse

Isaiah 1:18

Sidney Leasure

Object Lesson

Have each student make an animal of their choosing out of Play-Doh.

Point

Ask the students how they would feel if their animals came to life and refused to believe things they were told in order to protect them. For example: Their animals would not believe that they would harden if left out overnight. They also would not believe they would stain the carpet. The animals would act as if they were smarter than their creator. Explain to the students that we must recognize who we are compared to God. He is the creator, and we are His creation. We must be obedient to God's Word.

Verse

Isaiah 1:2-4

Object Lesson

Take a balloon and hold it to the wall, then ask, "Will the balloon stay?" The students will answer "no." Take the balloon and rub it in your hair, then stick it to the wall and it will stay.

Point

The balloon will not stick to the wall unless we add static electricity. We cannot do things that go against logic. But with faith, all things are possible. Faith is believing in things unseen. We must have faith in God and everything that He can do.

Verse

Matthew 17:20-21

Object Lesson

Get a piece of cardboard and cut a hole just big enough to get your fist through. Place a banana on the opposite side of the cardboard. Have someone stick their hand through the hole and grab the banana at the center, trying to bring the banana back through the hole without letting go of it.

Point

Explain that this is how monkeys are caught in the wild. The monkey will refuse to let go of the banana, even if it means he will get caught. Explain that, in our lives, this is how "pet sins" are. We will not let go of our pet sins, even if they bring bad news to our lives and we do them until we get caught. We must learn to get rid of pet sins.

Verse

Psalm 32:5

Object Lesson

Put a piece of paper inside a flashlight between the contact and the batteries. Turn on the flashlight, and after it will not work, open the flashlight, remove the batteries, and pull out all the trash from inside. Place the batteries back inside and then turn on the flashlight.

Point

Explain how we cannot let our light shine for Jesus if we have a lot of stuff in our life that "dulls out" our light. We are the bulb, and Jesus is our energy source. If we let the world come between us and our energy source, then our light cannot be seen. People cannot see Jesus within us if the world comes first, or if it comes between us and Jesus.

Verse

Ephesians 5:8-20

Object Lesson

Bring a rat trap and put some cheese on the trap. Then ask someone to stick their finger in the trap. After no one will volunteer to do this, walk around the room and snap the trap a couple of times.

Point

Explain how Satan entraps us with something desirable that looks good at the time, but he uses it to harm us. This lesson would be a good opportunity to talk to students about sex, drugs and alcohol.

Verse

I Peter 5:8-9

Object Lesson

Put a tea bag in a pot of hot boiling water and another tea bag in a pot of cold water. Watch as the tea bag in the hot water produces tea quickly, while the tea bag in the cold water is slow to respond.

Point

God sometimes allows trials to come to us so we will rely on Him more by faith — or sometimes just to produce more faith in our lives. Oftentimes, we need God to awaken us. The tea bag in the water is much like we are in our own lives: The hot water represents trials, while the cold water represents a life with no trials. The more trials we have in our life, the more we respond to God.

Verse

James 1:2-4, 1 Peter 1:6-7, Psalm 66:10

Object Lesson

Bring three tennis balls in a tennis ball can and a cup of rice. As you begin the devotion, fill the can with the rice first and then try to add the tennis balls, showing how they do not all fit. Next, empty the can and add the tennis balls first, then add the rice to the can. The tennis balls and the rice will then fit into the can.

Point

Explain how the tennis balls represent God, and the rice represents everything else in our daily lives. Explain that if God is put last in our lives, He will not fit into our lives. But if God is placed first in our lives, then everything fits together. God must come before all else if life is to work.

Verse

Matthew 6:33

Object Lesson

Place something rotten inside a box (rotten banana, moldy bread, etc.) and wrap with pretty giftwrap. Then wrap a nice gift inside a badly wrapped box. Pick two students and have one of them choose which gift they would like to open. Then allow the other student to open the other package.

Point

This will prove that the outside appearance does not show you what is on the inside. You cannot judge someone by their appearance or color of skin. Judge a man by the beauty of his heart. Talk how we are all different, and we should judge others by what's on the inside and not the outside. The outside can be deceiving as to what is inside.

Verse

I Samuel 16:7

Sidney Leasure

Object Lesson

Tell all the students who have a cell phone to start texting each other in the room. See how many texts they can send out within three minutes. Give the student who has texted the most a prize.

Point

Explain how prayer is just like texting others. We text random thoughts to random people continually. We just text whenever a thought hits us. Explain that this is how God wants us to pray. God wants us to talk to Him continuously with our random thoughts all day long and to keep in constant contact with Him.

Verse

1 Thessalonians 5:17

Object Lesson

Bring in a cake mix and follow the directions —
but instead of eggs use ketchup, and instead of oil
use jelly, and see what the batter looks like. Then
ask the students if they think the batter you made
will make a delicious cake. Make the point that you
must obey the instructions exactly when making
the cake. Then bring out a pre-baked cake.

Point

Share the story of Saul and how he disobeyed God
because he cowered to the voice of the people.
Tell the students how we must obey God to a tee,
and we must not cut corners. Explain how we must
guard ourselves to always obey God, even when we
are confronted with peer pressure.

Verse

I Samuel 15:7-23

Object Lesson

Place three cups on a table and fill the first cup halfway with water, labeling it "You." Next, fill the middle cup halfway with iodine, labeling it "Sin." Then fill the last cup halfway with bleach, labeling it "Christ."

Point

Pour some iodine into the water to show that we have sinned as the water turns dark. Then pour some bleach into the water and tell how Christ takes our sin away as the water becomes clear again. Pour some iodine into the bleach and explain how God placed the sin of the world on Jesus. Then pour some bleach into the iodine to illustrate how Jesus took all the sin from the world.

Verse

1 John 1:7

Object Lesson

Set out a scoop of lemonade mix next to an empty pitcher and ask who wants lemonade (looking like you are about to mix some up). Most of the kids will say yes. Then put a small amount of lemonade mix into cups and pass out the cups, telling the kids to drink up. Ask the kids why they are not drinking, and they will say, "You did not add the water." Pour the powder from each cup into the pitcher and mix up some lemonade.

Point

Explain to the students that, just as the lemonade is not lemonade without water, we, too, are not whole without the living water of Jesus Christ. Just as our bodies will die in three days without water, our souls will die without the water of Jesus Christ. Go into detail.

Verse

John 4:13

Object Lesson

(This lesson is to be performed outside.) Fill a small sour cream container three-fourths full of water, then add four Alka Seltzers and close the lid. Keep talking about anything in general as you wait for the lid to pop off of the container. It will catch the students off guard.

Point

Talk to them about how we must be able to control our anger, because it will act just as the container of Alka Seltzers did and blow up on people if we do not. God says it is not a sin to be angry; it is how we handle our anger that can become sin.

Verse

Ephesians 4:26

Object Lesson

Bring a GPS from your car to class. Explain how the GPS guides us, tells us where to turn, where to stop, and where to continue. It also warns us of road outages and dangers ahead.

Point

Explain that the Holy Spirit guides our life just as the GPS does our traveling. Explain how lost we can get without the Holy Spirit guiding us through life's highways. The Holy Spirit directs us and also warns us of dangers ahead in our lives. If we fail to follow the Holy Spirit's directions and we get lost, the Holy Spirit will redirect us out of trouble.

Verse

John 16:13-15

Object Lesson

Bring in a hammer. Ask the students what the hammer is used for.

Point

Explain how the hammer could be used to build something — or it could be used to tear something down. It either puts in a nail, or it pulls it out. God gives us all free will to choose His Son and eternal life, and to choose to do good or bad with our lives. We are each a different tool in His tool box, and it is up to us how we are used. We can build ourselves and others up — or we can tear ourselves and others down.

Verse

2 Timothy 2:21

Object Lesson

Bring in three flashlights — one bright, one dim, and one with no batteries. Turn on all three flashlights and show the difference in them.

Point

Jesus is the light of the world — and when He resides in us, His light should be seen in us. Are we like the flashlight without a battery that does not know Jesus? Are we like the flashlight that is dim by letting the world dim our light? Are we the bright light that allows everyone to see Jesus living within us? The way we live our lives determines the brightness of our light.

Verse

Matthew 5:14-16

Sidney Leasure

Object Lesson

Hold your cell phone up and ask the youth, "How do you get in touch with someone?" "Can you call someone by dialing any old number?" "Where do you get someone's number from?"

Point

Read Romans 10:12: "Everyone who calls on the name of the Lord will be saved." Explain that to be saved, we must call out to God, and we must know His number — which is "J-E-S-U-S." Just like the phone book, we get God's "phone number" from the Bible. Let the students know that God accepts phone calls at any time of the night. We can call out His name at any time.

Verse

Romans 10:12-13

Object Lesson

Bring ingredients to make a batch of cookies. Get each student to taste each ingredient separately. Let them taste the flour, the butter, the oil, the chocolate chips, etc. Then bake the cookies, or bring in some that have been already baked.

Point

Tell how some of the ingredients were not very good, but some were very tasty. That is how life is — there will be some bad times and some good times, but God can make all things work together for good.

Verse

Romans 8:28

Object Lesson

Tell the youth we are going to have a math lesson today to find out how much God loves us. So if A B C D E F G H I J K L M N O P Q R S T U V W X Y Z = 1 2 3 4 5 6 7 8 9 10 11 12 13 14 15 16 17 18 19 20 21 22 23 24 25 26, then find the sum of H+A+R+D+W+O+R+K = and K+N+O+W+L+E+D+G+E =. Then look at how much the L+O+V+E +O+F G+O+D = adds up to be.

Point

With mathematical certainty, we can then conclude that hard work and knowledge will only get you close to heaven — with 98 percent and 96 percent. Anything less than 100 percent is missing out on heaven. But the love of God will get you there with 101 percent.

Verse

Romans 5:8

Object Lesson

Bring in a picture of a horse following a carrot (you can find one on the internet). Show this to the class.

Point

The horse is fixated on the carrot and will follow that carrot all day and do all the work that his master needs without knowing he is a slave to his owner. We cannot become fixated on what this world has to offer and not realize we are slaves of the devil. We must have our eyes on Jesus and follow His will for our lives.

Verse

Hebrews 12:1-2

Object Lesson

God is absolute and maintains complete order. Do these math problems with a calculator to understand how exact God really is.

$1 \times 8 + 1 =$	$1 \times 9 + 2 =$
$12 \times 8 + 2 =$	$12 \times 9 + 3 =$
$123 \times 8 + 3 =$	$123 \times 9 + 4 =$
$1234 \times 8 + 4 =$	$1234 \times 9 + 5 =$
$12345 \times 8 + 5 =$	$12345 \times 9 + 6 =$
$123456 \times 8 + 6 =$	$123456 \times 9 + 7 =$
$1234567 \times 8 + 7 =$	$1234567 \times 9 + 8 =$
$12345678 \times 8 + 8 =$	$12345678 \times 9 + 9 =$
$123456789 \times 8 + 9 =$	$123456789 \times 9 + 10 =$

9 x 9 + 7 =	I x I =
98 x 9 + 6 =	I I x I I =
987 x 9 + 5 =	I I I x I I I =
9876 x 9 + 4 =	I I I I x I I I I =
98765 x 9 + 3 =	I I I I I x I I I I I =
987654 x 9 + 2 =	I I I I I I x I I I I I I =
9876543 x 9 + I =	I I I I I I I x I I I I I I I =
98765432 x 9 + 0 =	I I I I I I I I x I I I I I I I I =
987654321 x 9 + 0 =	I I I I I I I I I x I I I I I I I I I =

Point

God is a God of order in everything that He created, all the way down to numbers.

Verse

I Corinthians 14:33

Object Lesson

Get two students to volunteer. Let one wear an old, oil-stained T-shirt you brought in, and let the other wear a clean white T-shirt.

Point

Bring in the student with the stained T-shirt to illustrate the way we were before we were saved. Then bring in the student wearing the clean T-shirt to show how we look before God's eyes, once we have accepted Jesus Christ as our Lord and Savior. Then bring back the student wearing the stained T-shirt and tell how we like to go back and live like we are still wearing the stained T-shirt, when we should be trying to be more like Jesus and showing how clean God has made us.

Verse

Ephesians 4:17-24

Object Lesson

Bring in some pictures of the students from your youth group and tape them together on the wall. Then list on a sheet of paper different characteristics of God. Explain that an image is a reflection of someone or something. Tell how God made us in His image, including the characteristics listed.

Point

Discuss how God made us in His image, physically and character-wise, but sin has blurred that image. However, one man came to earth who was the exact image of God, and that was Jesus — and we must try to emulate Him.

Verse

Genesis 1:27, 2 Corinthians 3:18

Object Lesson

Bring pictures of a house, a car, a painting, and a flower.

Point

Ask the class what tools were needed to build the house, and then the car. Ask the class what was needed to make the painting. Then ask the class who and what was involved in making flowers grow. Describe to everyone how we are all tools in God's tool box, but He uses us all differently — and we should acknowledge how God uses us and not become jealous over other people's gifts. God has made us all good at something, which is usually different from someone else's gift.

Verse

I Corinthians 12:4-7

Object Lesson

Put a chalk pad or big paper tablet on an easel, and write a sentence with one misspelled word. After the students notice it and say something, pretend that you don't hear them. Next, argue that it is spelled right and have someone look it up in the dictionary. After you learn that it is spelled incorrectly, say that you have decided to spell it that way anyway. Next, agree that it is spelled wrong and cover it up with your hand. Finally, ask them what you should do about it. They should answer for you to rewrite the word correctly.

Point

Explain that this is the way we treat sin in our lives:

First — We pretend that we don't see it

Second — We argue that it is right

Third — We decide we do not care what the rules say; we are going to do it our way

Fourth — We agree it is wrong, but try to cover it up

However, God wants us to see our sins, recognize them, admit to them, turn away from them, make them right, and then ask for forgiveness.

Verse

1 John 1:9

Object Lesson

Get a mop head and pull the cords out of it to use as rope pieces. Give each student two pieces of rope and let them twist the pieces together. They will soon see how easily they come apart. Now give each person a third piece of rope and tell them to braid the three pieces together. Let them see how much harder it is to get them apart when three pieces are braided together, compared to two pieces.

Point

Explain to them that in any relationship where two people are joined together, as in a marriage, that the marriage is stronger when a third cord is added — and that third cord should be God. He can strengthen any marriage to where it cannot be pulled apart.

Verse

Ecclesiastes 4:12

Object Lesson

Get the youth to try to count the hairs on their head. After everyone fails at this, tell everyone to pull a piece of hair from their head and then cite Luke 12:7: "Indeed, the very hairs of your head are numbered."

Point

Explain how God knows each person very intimately. He knows how many hairs are on your head. Explain just how valuable each person is for God to know you so well. Then read Psalm 139: 1-18 slowly, making each verse personal to each student.

Verse

Psalm 139:1-18

Object Lesson

Bring a bag of M&Ms to class.

Point

Point out how the M&Ms are marked, just as we are marked with the seal of the Holy Spirit. M&Ms also comes in a variety of colors, just as we do. M&Ms are filled with chocolate — and we are filled with the sweet Holy Spirit and God's love. An M&M without the chocolate center is just a fragile, tasteless shell, as we are also just a fragile and empty shell without God within us.

Verse

Ephesians 4:30, I Corinthians 12:4-6, I John 4:12-15

Object Lesson

Bring two balloons — one blown up by yourself, and one filled with helium. The helium balloon represents us with God's Spirit within us; the other balloon represents us without God.

Point

The balloon that is blown up with air represents us trying to do all things without the Spirit of God. We always stay grounded, and we lie on the floor among the muck and dirt. The balloon with the helium is us being filled with the Holy Spirit. We rise above worldly things and find our way to heaven, with the Holy Spirit lifting us.

Verse

Philippians 4:13

Object Lesson

Bring a wrapped Christmas gift to class.

Point

Tell about God's gift to all of mankind, which includes each student. Describe how fun it is to give and see someone enjoy the gift they receive — and how God wants that feeling. You do not have to pay for the gift from God. It is a gift given freely with His love. Emphasize that the gift is for everyone. No one is excluded. The gift is not ours unless we stick out our hand and receive it. Explain how we must receive Jesus to be saved.

Verse

John 3:16, Ephesians 2:8

Object Lesson

Give each student a candy cane.

Point

Explain what the candy cane represents. The white is for the holiness of Jesus, for He was without sin. The white also is a picture of us after our sins have been washed away by the blood of Jesus. The red stripes represent the blood of Jesus that was shed for us, and the stripes are for when He was beaten. The hardness of the candy reminds us that Jesus is our rock. The candy cane's shape is that of a shepherd's staff that Jesus uses to keep and protect us. If you turn the candy cane upside down, you have a "J" for Jesus.

Verse

Hebrews 4:15, Isaiah 1:18, Isaiah 53:5, 1 Peter 2:6, John 10:11, Matthew 1:21

Object Lesson

Give all the students a plastic spoon and a small container of pudding. Tell the students to get a spoon full of pudding and try to eat without bending their elbows. They quickly find out it is impossible to eat without being able to bend your elbows.

Point

Tell them this story:

A man had a dream that he went to a place where there were two banquet rooms. In the first room, he saw a table filled with some of the most delicious food — but everyone sitting around the table was sad, and no one was eating. He noticed they could not bend their elbows, so they could not feed themselves. Then the man went to the second room, and there he also found a table filled with food and a room full of people who could not bend their elbows. However, they were all happy and eating. He noticed they were doing something that the other room was not doing: They were feeding one another. They could not get the food into their own mouths, but they could feed the person across the table from them. The first room was sad and hungry because they were selfish, but the second room was happy and satisfied because they were giving.

Have the students feed each other pudding without bending their elbows.

Verse

1 Peter 4:10

Object Lesson

Give each student a small, travel-size tube of toothpaste and a paper towel. Tell each student to squeeze out a portion of the toothpaste onto the paper towel. Then instruct the students to put the toothpaste back into the tube. They will tell you that it is impossible.

Point

Explain that the same is true about the things we say to others: Once we say hurtful words, we cannot take them back. Just like we cannot put the toothpaste back, we cannot return the words back inside of our mouths as if they were never spoken. Everyone has heard the rhyme "Sticks and stones may break my bones, but words will never hurt me." Well, that rhyme is far from the truth. Words do hurt very much. We need to be very careful about what we say to others.

Verse

Psalm 19:14

Object Lesson

Bring a picture of a caterpillar and a butterfly.

Point

Ask what correlation the two insects have in the pictures. Explain that when we are saved, we become a new person in Christ. We were once dirty and wretched, but now we are new and clean and beautiful in God's sight. Also explain that this is the reason we go through baptism — to show the world that our old selves have died and that we are now newborn creatures. Then explain how we will all get new bodies when we enter into heaven.

Verse

Romans 6:4, 1 Corinthians 15:44

Object Lesson

Bring a carved jack-o'-lantern to class.

Point

Explain that the jack-o'-lantern represents a newborn Christian. Lift the top off of the pumpkin and tell how, when we are saved, God opens us up and goes inside to clean us out. He removes the old, dirty, yucky insides that we were created with. God then disposes of the old stuff and leaves us with just a shell. He then resides in us, as does the candle inside the pumpkin, and He shines His light from within us just as the candle does. Then turn the pumpkin around and show the smiling face that is carved into the pumpkin, and tell how we are also smiling with joy with the presence of Jesus Christ inside of us. You can also explain how the carver personally picked out his pumpkin, just like God chooses us.

Verse

Psalm 51:10

Sidney Leasure

Object Lesson

This is a good lesson for Memorial Day. Bring in a cross, some nails, a large hammer, a whip, and any other object of the crucifixion that can be found.

Point

In remembrance of our Lord and Savior for what He sacrificed for all of us on the cross, go over each item in depth, telling what Jesus went through with each item. Explain the agony and how He did it for everyone in the room — and how He did it willingly. Explain the awesome love displayed on that day — and that we need to respond today, if we have not yet, to His calling.

Verse

Romans 5:6-10

Object Lesson

Have the students run some kind of race, whether it be a sack race, or a three-legged race, or just races around the church building.

Point

Read I Corinthians 9: 24-26 to the class after they have raced. Tell how athletes train with so much willpower and make so many sacrifices to play sports or to win races, just to receive a prize that will decay. Then explain what the real race is about: It is about making it through this life living for the glory of God. Tell the students that if we sacrifice for the real race, we will win the race and receive a prize much more valuable than a perishable trophy.

Verse

I Corinthians 9:24-26

Object Lesson

Have two sisters or brothers come up to the front of the class.

Point

Point out how they are family. Ask who in the room would get their father's inheritance and why. (Answer: The siblings would, because they are family.) Could you just walk into one of the sibling's houses at night and claim a bed for yourself? No, because you are not part of their family. You may know the father of the siblings, but that does not count. Then relate how we must be part of God's family to get His inheritance and to move into His house (heaven) — and that just knowing Him is not enough. Emphasize to the students how to join the family of God.

Verse

Ephesians 2:19

Object Lesson

Take the students to your car and let one of them sit in the driver's seat.

Point

While one student is sitting in the driver's seat of your car, explain how God should sit in the driver's seat of our lives. He should be driving our car in life, and we should go along for the ride. We should not worry about the destination, but instead enjoy where we are being taken. Then let a student sit in the back seat and explain that too many times we drive our car, decide our own destination, and have God ride in the back seat — where He has no input on our destination. He is back there for us to talk to occasionally, but we give Him no control of our daily lives. Then have a student sit in the trunk of your car and explain that this is where most Christians put God in life. God rides in their trunk. This way we do not have to talk to God or communicate with Him in any way unless we have an emergency. We use God as if He is a spare tire. We use Him only long enough to carry us until we can fix the problem ourselves, and then we put God back in the trunk and forget about Him until we have another emergency. Ask the students: "What type of Christian are you?" and "What do you need to change in your life to allow God to drive your car?"

Verse

Psalm 73:24

Object Lesson

Get the students to name characteristics of a pig and a cat.

Point

Talk how pigs love the mud. Share how pigs will wallow and sit in the mud all day, and then walk around with the mud caked onto their bodies. In contrast, a cat hates the mud. Have you ever seen a cat get its paws dirty and try to shake them in the air as it walks? It cannot stand to get wet or dirty. A cat will sit for hours lying on the floor, giving itself a bath. Then explain to the students that this is much like the difference between someone who is saved and someone who is not. The unsaved man loves sin and thinks it is fun, just as the pig loves mud. A saved man hates sin, just like the cat hates to have muddy paws. He desperately regrets getting dirty from sin and tries to separate himself from the dirt and does not want to do it again.

Verse

Romans 6:6-7, I John 5:4-5

www.ingramcontent.com/pod-product-compliance
Lightning Source LLC
Chambersburg PA
CBHW071431040426
42445CB00012BA/1346